Bhagavad Gita An Answer for Life!

Vishnuvarthanan Moorthy

i

ISBN:1512182796
ISBN-13:9781512182798

DEDICATION

To The Supreme Power

" He creates, He maintains, He destroys and He Authors!"

iv

CONTENTS

Introduction   viii

1   The Yoga of Arjuna's Grief   Pg 1

2   The Yoga of Knowledge   Pg 8

3   The Yoga of Action   Pg 18

4   The Yoga of Renunciation of Action   Pg 25

5   The Yoga of True Renunciation   Pg 31

6   The Yoga of Self Control   Pg 34

7   The Yoga of Wise Understanding   Pg 37

8   The Yoga of Indestructible Brahma   Pg 39

9   The Yoga of Royal Secret   Pg 42

10 The Yoga of Divine Glories   Pg 47

11 The Yoga of Cosmic Form   Pg 52

12 The Yoga of Devotion   Pg 59

13 The Yoga of the Field and it's Knower   Pg 63

14 The Yoga of the Three Gunas   Pg 68

15 The Yoga of Supreme Being   Pg 72

16 The Yoga of Divine and Demonic   Pg 76

17   The Yoga of Three Fold Faith   Pg 80

18   The Yoga of Moksha by Renunciation   Pg 84

     Conclusion   Pg 88

INTRODUCTION

Bhagavad Gita - For many it's highly respected life science or way of living or just a fictional book or a Hindu's guidebook for life, "hmm", there are lots of such perspectives and everyone like to see it in the way in they wants to see it. There have been many books published on this with adequate details and various views given by various Saints & Scholars. However here, in front of you - one more view! As a common person, who lives among the 500+ crore people, searching still the identity for himself and his life, I present the understanding, which I get by reading those complex words and trying to decode them.

Why should I? - This is the first question I had, when I started this journey. "It should be me"- that is what my heart said and here I am. I, born in this world, like anyone else, was introduced to Bhagavad Gita as a great holy book by parents and teachers. I have the belief that there is a reason for everything and including my birth, this could be mostly the same for all the readers here! I, who is working in an IT company, can access to a richer lifestyle as I demand, but by birth, I am from normal Indian family and by caste or by nature not so religious. However, changes and situations in life made me feel there is nothing more than a superior power in this world and every living and non-living being is controlled by that. With that belief, I lead my daily life! My reading of Gita is to understand, what is that the supreme power has communicated to humankind and to me and to you! I believe it is my right to understand and decode Gita on my own way (as I am a component of that supreme power) and to share with the ones who are interested in taking those views. Gita is not for storing in Pooja room or in your library . God told Gita for you and me, for us to understand and lead our normal life and perform our duty! (Saints can give clarifications, but it is not for them, as they do not have much to achieve in this world! God told Gita to a warrior, to do his duty and not for a saint!)

Let us begin our experience!

1 THE YOGA OF ARJUNA'S GRIEF

Brief Background:

Let us understood from where and why the Bhagavad Gita comes in, before we are in to chapter one details. The Bhagavad Gita is a part of Mahabharata - the epic. In which the supreme personality of god has taken the form of "Krishna" and born in world. In this incarnation, God remained with God Qualities but with human form. Mahabharata is a story about a kings family, in which the cousins (with their family) trying to establish hold in the kingdom, whereas few with rightful and few with greediness intent. It shows many of the characters which we are still seeing in our normal life. It ends in battlefield where Kauravas (the misguided ones) and Pandavas (the rightful ones) stand on opposite side to settle scores. Krishna is with Pandavas as they asked for him and Krishna's soldiers are with Kauravas as they asked for them.

Characters to Know:

Krishna: He is the Supreme Personality of God. We can call as the supreme power. He is uncle to the Pandavas and Kauravas. He has nothing to gain or lose in the battle (why do we say that- will see in coming chapters)

Arjuna: He is the Mighty Archery man and one of the Pandavas. Arjuna is very close to Krishna and they both share a relationship, which has no category. It is pure form of love, affection and respect.

"Our life: Do we ever try not categorizing our love or anyone's love at any time.... No, always we need some form like a friend, sister, mother, uncle, wife, daughter, etc... Unless we compare and categorize we can't accept the love and affection in a formless way... may be the common man is more rule oriented and pattern oriented"

Remember Arjuna is not someone else, "he is me and you", and he represented us in front of Krishna. Every human being who reads this is Arjuna, with whom the god has spoken. Let me scope it out, Gita is written only for human and his purpose only! In addition, for other living beings (animals, birds, plants, etc.) there could be something, which we are not aware of... Similarly, it was told to a man, so the grammar always follows the singular pointers to male; however, the woman has to apply applicable grammar when they read.

Sanjaya: He is the person who was able to see all the happenings on the battlefield with his exceptional power and who is explaining to Dhritarashtra (the king). He is the reason for us to know what is there in Gita or what God has said to Arjuna, we could call him "The Remote Hearing/Visual Aid"

Dhritarashtra: He is the King and father of Kauravas. He was blind and he was not there in the battlefield, but trying to understand, what is going on through Sanjaya.

Opening:

Sanjaya is explaining to Dhritarashtra, that is what is happening on the battlefield. He could see that millions of soldiers are in an array on both sides. The greatest warriors and relatives on both the sides are standing there with their chariots and weapons to conquer each other. *"Our Life: I used to see lots of English movies, so I remembered The Mummy, lord of the rings, Alexander, etc. and trying to imagine, what could be the magnitude of such military, Wow... It is Excellent for imagination! But remember they were living human, each one had a family and every life had a history, I and you could be one among the soldier who left his wife in the house and thinking , we will return back in a few days with life. We always think about ourselves as hero or villain, and why not as a side actor!"*

Krishna was driving Arjuna's cart with a purpose. Why does god drive a cart? The fact is he was driving the battlefield, which was going to teach the human - what life is all about! ...

Chapter for Dummies:

Arjuna wants to see who all are there in battlefield to fight along with him and against him, in that battle. This is like, self-stocktaking and to see what is going on. He asked Krishna to take the cart in between both the militaries to have a better view. Krishna then took the cart to the centre of the field and told Arjuna on his both sides, he can see his soldier's and of his opponents.

"Our life: We like to imagine India-Pakistan, US-Russia or ourselves and an unfriendly neighbor or colleague in the workplace and imagine that we are the good ones and others are our opponents. We don't have the guts to think, that one side is my impure characteristics and the other side is my pure characteristics and god has placed the cart in between them, and asking me to see both the sides of me. Let's try to do that and perform the stock taking!

We all have three level of response system with us, a) the outer one - the "survival" system, which responds in a good or bad way ,as it's been habituated by the person based on the environment he/she lived, it's more of immediate actions b) the inner one - the "planning" system, which is based on mind and heart, the good and bad here is born after analysis, they have long standing effect (we all might be talking to ourselves with our mind &heart), by the way "Heart can never talk/think"- but it's a notion for love, affection, kindness and truthful thinking of Mind c) The Supreme Inner one- the "Purest Soul", we interact rarely in our day to day activities with this one, this is pure and can never be modified (no good and bad in this level) , but on constant practice (ex: Yoga/meditation/self realization) we can interact with that. This tells at any time "Are we doing right in life"!

Now coming back, imagine now- we are looking from the purest soul perspective the way the other two layers are working with us- the good and bad responses."

Arjuna had a look, he can see only his uncle, ancestors, teachers and well-wishers on either side and he could not understand, who his real enemies out there are, as he was confused by the relationship and attachment he has with them. He tells Krishna, Even if someone gives me the three worlds, I will not kill them to attain it. I am not here as greedy, who kills his own people to achieve something and I will not be able to take the sin that arises out of this act.

As a common person, we can say, Arjuna was good and he is not ready to put down his family for the price of land. In addition, Arjuna is seeking peace and there is nothing wrong with it?

"Our Life: For most of us, peace is something important. According to us, ' peace' is something, which is normal life without any change and not getting into any new position, or it is a position of making no decision. The fact is, being ignorant of most of the happenings in the surroundings and self is what many a time we do for this peace. If we do not raise our voice against social discrimination, discrimination, family or any level, we live in peace, if this is our way of peace, then it is called "ignorance". We like to do that, because we do

5

not want to take decisions in our life and we do not want to lose anything in life (attachment & relationship to something). This is exactly what Arjuna felt."

Arjuna goes on and says to Krishna, instead of doing such a sin of killing my own men and get the sin, which will affect my life and all members in the family, I would rather go to battlefield without any armour and die at the hands of Kauravas. He put is his bow and sat down in the cart.

Arjuna has concluded, what is good and what is not good and what will fetch him sin and everything. His conclusion was based on his understanding and knowledge on, what is good.

"Our Life: The results coming out of an activity are classified by us good and bad, and they are decided so, by the community rule, a situation, point of view, etc. The human eye cannot see clearly anything, which is far and can see only the things that are nearer, the same way his rules are based on the closer things, which he sees, live and believe. It does not mean all others are untrue. Just because we do not see a microorganism in our bare eye, it does not mean there is nothing! We see movies and we get emotional, don't we know that is untrue! Nevertheless, that is human and he is driven by emotions, illusions and desires! Human thinks, he is the wisest of all and he knows what is right and what is wrong! Nevertheless, the reality is he does not know himself and his purpose! Like Arjuna, we also have our own understanding on what's good/right and bad/wrong, and it's only based on our

region/religion/society/belief, the same for another human from a different region/religion/society/belief could mean differently"

2 THE YOGA OF KNOWLEDGE

As Arjuna has put down his bow and sat down, Krishna started talking to him. Krishna asked Arjuna, from where he is bringing this weakness at this difficult situation, in which, Arjuna has to perform his duty as a warrior. Krishna went ahead and told, by doing such an act, he will not achieve heaven nor do any fame and he ask Arjuna to leave such weakness behind and perform his duty. Arjuna replied to Krishna, that he would not do such an act, which can kill his nearer and dearer, after that, he became silent.

"Our Life: Arjuna's weakness came from attachment and fear of the unknown, it's the same for us, and we all have our weakness towards losing any attachment. Be it a car, relationship, home or anything - we do not want to lose and we are not ready for anything unexpected. We all want favorable condition throughout life. We pray to God always bless us with favorable conditions. The other fact is, we do not know, how to manage

an unfavorable condition or an event. Our parents or elder in our life do not teach us, how to manage a death/lose/fear, but they only tell us to think always in favorable positives. In an unfavorable condition, most of us fail or get anxious/ worried/stressed and not able to come out of it. Basically we have never been taught on how to manage the loss of something (everything is taken from here and one day they will go off)"

After listening to Arjuna, Krishna has smiled and started speaking those words, which are going to be the underlying principles for living and non-living beings in the world and across universes. Krishna has told Arjuna, that he is grieving for which, he should not. He said, as human changes the dress on a daily basis, the soul also changes its body. The soul, which is born in this world with a body, over a period, will leave the body through death, and will again take the new body and will born.

"Our life: We all know, every day new cells are born and old cells die in our body. The birth and death take place in our brain, heart, hand and everywhere. Yet, we are not aware of! Because it has taken care by the supreme power! For many of us, it is science! (Now if your friend or wife says, that you are not the same as of yesterday, you can accept with smile)"

Krishna went ahead and told Arjuna, the wise man will take pleasure and pain the same way, the body is perishable can't be protected , but the soul is imperishable and no one can cause destruction to them.

"Our Life: If a farmer thinks, he shouldn't remove a

blossoming flower from the plant, he is ignorant, and the flower will be perished on its own. However the same farmer thinks, the soul of the plant could be destroyed, that is not possible, because the soul takes the next birth. Now I have a question, if 10000 years before if the world had only thousands of human , then only the same count of soul will be there, but how come today, we have 500 crore people , it means 500 crore souls , how the new souls came in ?... oops... no... I got the answer, the soul count includes animals and plants also, we destroyed so many of them, and they are born among us to teach a lesson to us :)"

Krishna told Arjuna; whoever thinks that they kill the soul, is ignorant. The soul is not newly created and it's never destructed but they attach to a body, based on the attachments they gained. The soul which has carried the goodness/sins/desire/etc takes the body/form (animal/plant/human/etc.) it deserves , but the soul which never carries anything, but has only the supreme personality of God as the goal, will not born with a body, but will stay with god. The soul can never be fired/burnt/wetted/cut or be in to any destruction. If this truth, you are only killing the body and not the soul. For something born here, death is certain. For something dead here, birth is certain.

It is like PMBOK/ ISO/ Global standard definition for the term "Project": Every project has Start and End :)

"Our Life: Don't we know we will die at some time. Yes, we all know, but at least for me it will not be near, maybe for Sam, John, or Raghu that could be early! , we

are happy to think like this. We always believe that we will live 70 years minimum. Who gave us the guarantee? Ok... let it is... Even having this Guarantee, what do we do? We want to study engineering or MBA or CA, etc., get a big salary, buy 1 or 2 houses and pay installments, have 1 or 2 kids, search for schools, run for college seats, pension plan, good four wheeler, full of loan (when we pay out a loan, we go for next loan) and son or daughter stays in far away city/country, deposit money in a senior citizen plan and one day get admitted in hospital! (Some of them think back and feel, they never did what they wanted and they lived such a poor life) This the life 400 + crore people living and in the past most of them had similar life... So who are we? Do you know , someone who lived in Mumbai (in Dadar) in some bungalow, 25 years back or someone lived in a palace in Rajasthan in A.D 1247 ... We don't know.. We do not know our purpose of life! Nevertheless, we all want this body to be there for minimum 70 years with us. To do what? I do not say that we have to be a historical personality or a popular person... Do we know, how many literatures & languages are lost, how many great people are unknown, do we know anyone who lived 12000 B.C, etc., No ... Even history and fame also goes away with the time. It is all about understanding that this body is not owned by us, and do not get attached to it, but only to our soul. That will lead us to a birthless state, however it doesn't mean, not to perform the duty, but not to get attached to worldly things and relationships, beyond a limit (self realized state -where we can separate as we demand)"

Krishna told Arjuna, the duty of a warrior is to fight and by not fulfilling his duty, he will achieve sin. The world will not appreciate the one, who has turned down his duty, and people may think because of fear he left the battlefield. By killing these bodies of the greedy one, you will fulfill you duties and may achieve the rightful position. Krishna went ahead and told the one who treats pleasure and pain, gain or loss, victory and defeat, alike will not achieve sin, because he performs his duty and he is not gaining anything out of the result and he is not bothered on result.

"Our Life: Performing duty, according to us, limit's to our family and our job. Most of us do not bother anything outside our life. Fulfilling our needs is a part of duty but that is not all! We do not give our voice for anything! Sorry, we do... We all talk to our friends, family about injustice/scam/social needs/changes to make in country, etc., and we believe strongly that someone will do the job for us (Perhaps we have faith in others, more than self-do). We go behind popular social causes, and we take road and we walk with candlelight, but we forget to step into our next door and stop the discrimination happening there. We talk about what happens in Srilanka and in Delhi, but we do not talk and take action on what happens in the nearby community or street. Beyond this, how many of us think that we need to keep the environment clean outside our house, how many of us dare to question a person who is polluting the society/economy/politics/health/environment, etc... Rare...But we all are duty conscious... We run for our bus, we run for our work, we run for our sleep and we

run for everything...but only for us and only for what we need !!!"

Krishna has started speaking about yoga to Arjuna, The one, who is resolute has a single mind of determination, the one who does not have his mind following different branch of thoughts and will be inconclusive and confused. The Resolute understands that everything here is taken from here and one day he will need to leave all this and go. He understands that all the beings here will change over a period and they are destroyable.

"Our Life: Most of us actually are living in simulation more than really current happening. How much we talk with our mind! How much we talk to others in our mind! How much we create people and their behaviours in our mind! We pre-decide about what the other person will talk, when we say something! We pre-decide what the situation will be when we enter an office/function/etc. It means we spend a huge amount of time in simulation, and many of them simulate the long future... They think, what will happen in their life, what money they would have earned, etc.... Neither they live in current nor do they live in the future. Some simulate the past and think, if this could have been that way, which would have been nice! The mind lays out branches for us to travel, but it's up to us to cut those branches and live in the present and be determined only about the supreme power or connected to our soul and perform actions without expectation on result"

Krishna told Arjuna that Veda's (holy rules) can guide a person to reach the demigods (Sun, moon, other forms of gods) and to get a good life, however the one who has attained the Yogic state is not pleased with them nor impressed by the power it gives. He who is in Yogic state can control the senses and still be living a normal life. When he meets the supreme power, he also loses the worldly interests and reaches the god without any obstacles. For that yogic person, Veda's serve no purpose.

"Our Life: We have seen, most of us don't understand Veda's clearly and their purpose. There are few, who has learnt Veda's, but I am not including them here... Most of us do many ceremonies/rituals in our house/temple without knowing the purpose, but with the belief it is god's language or ceremony and he will be pleased with that. We always forget, that solely thinking about him in our mind/heart and perform our duty, will please him more than anything will! However, the truth is we believe rituals alone will bring peace and harmony to our family and us. How untrue is this! We also see, there are some VIP's/rich people who enter in to temple/church/mosque and get high priority for them and get some good words from the priests and they think that god has blessed them. God is equal for every living being here and no need of any mediator here (the concept of Guru is different) and the importance given to them is a manual happening and it is not from god. The first thing, believe your god is knowledgeable. Do not think he can be fooled! Similarly, we see some temples/churches/mosques getting high donations; I am sure more the money comes from Sin and as part of the share for the Sin. We believe god will reduce our

punishment, if we give him some share"

Krishna told Arjuna, being in Evenness in success and failure is Yoga and yogic state. The one who performs the actions given to him, without worries/interests in the result, is actually getting into the Yogic state. He is not bothered about the fruitive result and he is in steady state. The one, who is self satisfied for what he is! He is in steady wisdom.

"Our Life: How many of us feel, till date we had very good life without any hassles, and how many feel, my life is the best! Not many... we still look at some other's life as the best life, we still look at someone as best person. We still need something else to make us satisfied. If I remember the movie "castaway", that showed a man who nearly attained self-satisfaction in the island, but that is more by force of nature and not by a wish. No materialistic things will leave you to be on your own and will make you as self-satisfied person on your own. Just, we need to leave them! There are many among us, who cannot live without a phone, who cannot live without TV, who cannot live without friends, who cannot live without something... Attachment to things, makes us comfortable and they do not let us think whom we are! We all are very comfortable, by not allowing ourselves to know, who we are and what we are doing... We need more internal control, to start thinking about ourselves...Sit somewhere quietly and think who you are... again don't think, what Sam and Raghu does in your life and don't think how your wife/son/parents behaves with you... it should be only you! There is

nothing more beautiful than you in god's creation and there is nothing holier than you in god's creation!"

Krishna went ahead and told Arjuna, when we are subjected to the senses and allow them to dominate, the attachments come, from the attachments we get the desire , from unfulfilled desire/broken desire the anger comes, from anger the delusion comes, from delusion we get confused in memory and we lose reasoning and that leads to ruin.

In that chain of speech, I can remember holy Buddha stating similar words...by the way; all these are more or less same, because the truth is single.

"There are no three or four gods in the world, neither so many of them rule this world. It is one supreme power, which has created and maintains this universe and other universes and even the microorganisms. In addition, that supreme power is Krishna! If you think, this is what I am going to say, I am sorry! This could be Nabhi, Jesus, or anyone, but there is a supreme power. Just because in my region (correlated with religion), we believe in the form of Krishna, I call him as the supreme power, but if am born in Saudi or in Italy, I will call him differently. Never Krishna crossed and went to Rome, nor Nabhi went New Zealand, nor did Jesus go to Vietnam. The religion and rituals are born from the region and conditions, however it does not mean there is no god. There is one supreme power, which is beyond imaginable knowledge, and power, which runs everything. The sad part of human is, unless he understands something, he believes they are not true.

Before Edison, no one knows about electricity, the older generation would have thought about him as a fool, but now electricity is a subject with few marks...Just because we don't see something/hear something/feel something, we can't say there is nothing... it's our limitation .... It's beyond science, its belief... that's the only way to see the god!"

3 THE YOGA OF ACTION

Arjuna asked Krishna, you are saying knowledge of Yoga is superior to Action, if so, by knowing this, why should I do the action of killing? In addition, he conveyed to Krishna that his speech seems to be conflicting in nature and no way is clear. Krishna replied to Arjuna, there are two ways, one is living in knowledge of yoga and another one is following the path of action of the yogis. Just by not performing an action, you would never reach Action-less state, nor by waivering your action you would achieve the perfect state. None of the living being at any instant remains inactive. The nature- born qualities are always working on them.

Let us clarify something, the word "Yoga" given here is not the breathing exercise taught or physical exercise taught in a "Yoga Class". It is a condition of maintaining evenness to the action, results and happenings, and living with self-consciousness.

Anyways, here we are not going to give any definitions of terminology, if at all, it is only for clarifications purpose.

"Our Life: The moment when someone decides (Yes, many of us decide, that now I will follow god religiously or now I will do additional charity, etc.) to follow supreme personality of god, they buy a book like Bhagavad Gita and starts reading it or watch television channels or attend religious meetings, then some of them conclude, everything in this world is untrue and there is no meaning in continuing working/doing duty, and they start to behave so weird, that their family members get really irritated and feels, why do this person get into it! Some of us do not keep Gita in our house, we do not keep Krishna and Arjuna's (together in the Battlefield) picture in our house, because we fear that will not help normal life and it will bring war in the house. Truth is Gita tells us how to live in evenness in normal life. Nevertheless, our understanding on evenness always goes on the extreme side, where we are not clear what to lose and what to control. Like Arjuna got confused at this moment, we also get confused by half understanding/knowledge"

Some of us attempt or perform meditation and some believe this is what an action less state. Meditation what we perform in normal life, can help us break our thoughts and make us concentrate, which might reduce the blood pressure and support the bodily happenings for a few minutes. However, once we finish our meditation, we search for our phones, we attend mails, we start arguments, etc. (we resumed normal life) ... This is where the meditation is required. It is nothing but, unattached to the action and to its result, but keep performing the action. A mind keep practicing this, is in real "meditation". Not the mind that repeats some word for 15 to 30 minutes, and comes back to normal senses and drives us crazy.

Krishna told Arjuna, controlling the senses by organs is not the right one, but controlling the mind over the objects of senses is the superior way. The one, who can restrain the senses by mind, involves his organs of action in Karma-Yoga, without attachment and he excels. The one who performs his duty by action and he is superior to the one who is inactive.

"Our Life: Many of us has different habit's which we our-self don't like, for example , we want to get up early on daily basis, but when we try to get up, we feel - why not another 15 min sleep... then we slip into sleep. Similarly, someone may want to quit smoking, but cant... this is because; we initiate controls with our senses and not with our mind. The senses are powerful; however, the mind is more powerful than senses. Mind thinks on consequences, where as senses cannot. Therefore, it is practically easier to control mind, which in turn will control the senses. In our mind when we fix up a time to get up, we do not need an alarm, on the exact time, we will get up. I am sure; many of us are experiencing this. But when it's not fixed in mind, even if the alarm rings, we will shut it"

Krishna told Arjuna, that actions has consequences ,

which has to be sacrificed (the result), that's the way one can do actions, The other way is for the one, who is self satisfied in self itself, for him there is no action is required, as he is not dependent on anything. He is not attached even to the actions (not only to the result). However, he also performs his duty (without attachment on actions). He told Arjuna, for the supreme god (Krishna himself) there is nothing to achieve in this world or in heaven or hell, but still he also is performing the duty without attachment.

"Our Life: I always have this question, even you might be having the same, Why should god make me born in this world and suffer here, and what is he trying to prove here, if I am not born here I would have been happy....Hmm... I never got any proper answer from anyone and I do not believe an answer logically (logic to an extent, we can understand) can be given here! God performs his duty of creation, maintenance and destruction of living beings in a materialistic environment, without any attachment and without any results in his mind, he is keeping doing it. However the living beings born here, is not able to live without any attachment and they enjoy taking pleasure and one day when there is pain, they ask question to God, why you make me born? (When we are very happy, we do not ask this!) We ask what is the result, god tries to achieve? Whereas, he already told us, this is his duty and he is not expecting result. However, for our logic, without a result why should he do? This is our question and we go ahead and think why cannot he stop doing his action? First, we want god to be attached to result then

attached to his action else, we want him to stop the action! The only problem here is we do not do our duty in the way he is telling us and now we want him to be attached to everything! God has also told a way to come out this birth and death, that's by being yogic and continue to be determined on supreme power, by that we can come out of this! But we are not ready for that, but we would like to advise god also"

Krishna told Arjuna, that the wise man, who understands that actions have to be performed without attachments, keeps performing it. However, they shouldn't unrest the one, who is ignorant, by giving partial/untakeble knowledge or understanding and make them confused. This will only create disorder! Every living being performs the actions based on the characteristic they have! The senses utilize them to act! The wise man knows how to manage it! In addition, one should not enter in to another one's duty and perform it, that should be avoided and it's unacceptable. He told Arjuna, as the fire is surrounded by smoke, the wisdom is always surrounded by desire, and hence the wise should be aware and remove the desire by control on mind and by concentrating on supreme power.

"Our Life: In life, we have to give something to others, only to an extent they can take and not beyond their limit. If everyone is capable of everything, the world would be having only robotic living. There will be no demand and supply. If everyone is a medical practitioner or construction engineer, the world will not run in a normal way. The world has its own cycle and everyone

here performs the role, which they have selected. However the one, who understand the importance of the role and how to be unattached with the role, can provide guidance to the other, based on the amount the other one can take it. However, going beyond a limit and feeding the one (who cannot take), will only create confusion! A construction worker , who is plastering the wall in 25th floor, hanging in a rope between sky and earth , is been told with all this and if he is asked to perform his duty without attachment, can he take it ?!! May be or may not be! (Do not think he cannot) The work he is doing does not qualify his characteristics and thinking, there could be few who can, few who cannot ...It depends on the individual. However, when they can't, then all you spoke with that person can only create disorder to his life! Similarly, no one can take decision for others (rightfully)! You cannot for your wife/son/husband/parents/friend, etc (rightfully)! No one can lead others (rightfully)! We are not been given the right, nor are we capable of! Most of them time, people who like to decide for others are worried to take a decision for them self (may be they like to pilot on others :))! We can only guide and give relevant support, but decision & action to be owned by the relevant individual and interfering in that is a Sin. However, when it is comes to a country/group/team the decisions are taken by selected individual; however it is a role that they play and it is their duty. Their credit's on life are purely depends on the decisions taken and duty performed as in that role!

Be the leader, when no one is ready to lead! Be the

decision maker, when no one is ready to decide! You can exclude this, only when it's a duty assigned to you!"

4 THE YOGA OF RENUNCIATION OF ACTION

Krishna told Arjuna, I have taught this Yoga to the Sun god, millennium's ago and he taught to others, by that many of them carried away it, as part of tradition, but over a period of time the chain was broken. So here I am, again giving you that knowledge.

Arjuna asked Krishna that you were born among us how did you teach this to sun god, because you seem to be lesser age than he is. Krishna replied Arjuna, that you are born many times and I am also born many times, and whenever in these worlds the righteousness reduces and unrighteous things grow, I born (as incarnation) with my Maya to destruct the wicked and protect the good and to establish dharma (truth/ fairness and kindness).

"Our Life: There are 10 incarnations of Vishnu, as told in Hindu mythology and one among them is Krishna and the last one still pending is "Kalki", in which the god

will come in "white horse with a sword" Hmm....
Interesting part is the initial few incarnations, which
were millions of year apart; the forms are like fish, pig
and turtle, etc. Why in the world, he is not in human
form? Did human race exist in that period? May not be
... Until I saw the movie Jurassic park, I was not aware
of dinosaurs. Now they are not in this world for many
thousand years... It means the world undergoes
change/revamp in a period... Today we get petrol in gulf,
under the dessert. The petrol existence means there was
rich organic elements were there in that place thousands
of years ago... Today only dessert exists. The world has
undergone huge amount of changes, which we are still
studying... Therefore, it means some revamping happens
on certain Intervals and human form may not have
existed at that point in time. Apart from this, I don't
know , whether for "Kalki", god will come in horse or he
will come with a new cyclone /series of earth
quake/volcano erupt/virus/bomb etc called "Horse" ,
who knows!!! When our Laptop is hung, what do we do,
we "Restart", similarly a machine is not working, what
we do, we "Restart", maybe we got this principle from
him :)"

Krishna told Arjuna, the one who knows this and who is
free from anger and fear, and free from attachment,
is absorbed by me and become one in me. The wise
performs action without any attachment.

"Our life: How do I know, I am without any attachment?
Hmm. Thing 3 thinks which you like the most in this life
(relationship/material/ or any). Ok... Now if we remove

those 3 from your life from tomorrow on wards, will you still have interest in life or do you inclined to live ? .. For many of us, it's "no". The one which you like the most, if you are ready to leave any time for its good or with the understanding of god , it means you are already living detached. Be clear, it includes fame/desire/etc also. Leaving the one which you like the most (including self), if you can do, then you have nothing to achieve here in this world. Now, I am writing all this, whether I am a saint, no ... Can I leave everything and live normally my life? I do not know... However, I am sure understanding that they are perishable can help me to live in a better way and handle things better way! "

Krishna told Arjuna, the one who can see action in inaction and inaction in action, is the wise. He is not attached to actions. The one who has removed the desire from actions and its results, have great wisdom and no sin can affect, when he performs the action. He lives with, what is the minimum needed for his life.

"Our Life: I see many a times, people start every activity in professional life with personal results in mind and only that as major target. Everyone has expectation in self, and the organization has his or hers, so we plan and agree what to achieve in a year. When it comes to self-goal, I see people start the year with the goal "promotion", "double-digit increment" etc... they go and ask the supervisor, what if I do, I will get them this year...They don't ask, what should I learn this year, they don't ask, what do you think is my potential and how can I use it for my duty effectively... People

employed in the current generation, only for their competency to do the job and the performance, instead of concentrating on improving the competency, people target on promotions and salary as the only goal! Their entire sets of actions are dependent only on that! It could be because they do not believe that their action will lead result or could be fear, that they may not achieve the result, or they only bothered about short-term goals! A confident, self-known person will not worry about the result, but will concentrate on the action... When you perform the activities in competent way, with evenness in your mind, the salary and promotions will come in your way... if not in this organization, it will be in the other :) but do not loose you, because you are precious and difficult to find, if you lose!

Anyone who is having assets more than what is required for his normal day to day life and for his emergency, is again attached to the materialistic nature. The materialistic things will not leave him. For him, nothing is adequate. Believe, even if he has 300 million plus dollars, he is going to say, it is inadequate for emergency, because by that time his asset will make him as servant (developed all kind of bondages like investment, loan, status, etc) and it will bring all the vulnerabilities to him. In windows operating system, when you try clean up the programs, it will show how frequently you use that program and it will tell you remove programs based on that. Similarly, when you actually don't use many of the things, asset is a curse"

Krishna went ahead and told Arjuna, through sacrifices

people try to achieve the almighty, some of them sacrifice material, some sacrifice hearing, some sacrifices senses, some practices breathing, some follow austerity, some follow regulated food and through them they try to destroy the sins. Above all, superior is knowledge about supreme and actions without attachments, you will learn this from the Guru's who has obtained such knowledge. The knowledge will act as fire to destroy all the desires. There is no purifier better than the soul of a knowledgeable person, who understands self and satisfied by self. The one, who is doubtful of this, will have happiness in either this world or in any other world.

"Our Life: Guru's (teacher) help us learn various practices and impart knowledge to us on different topics. The help of teacher and its requirement varies from person to person. Not everyone needs to attend religious classes or others. The need can only be determined by the self and not by others. Many of us in India follow gurus, which help for many, in concentrating and taking life forward. People take things, to the level, it is required for them. Be clear, there is nothing purer than your own soul and it has to be your goal to connect with it. Now a days , we see the so called gurus' have become business people and they have lot of things to maintain like publicity, assets, brand names, chain hospitals/restaurants/colleges, etc, donation inflow, organizational strength and sale of products. They want to sit in golden chair, some singer will be singing about them, and they listen happily talking about yours and my life. I am not pulling any one's leg, they will have their

own reason, as long as they are unattached to their actions and they do not have any expectations on results, we are no one to judge!

A guru guides you in a path, but the path only you have to walk. If you are dependent on a guru throughout your life, it means you have not walked, you are just standing there!

When you decide on something and on some person, never allow the doubt to come in your mind. That can destroy you. Before you decide on anything analyze and decide, but once you are engaged in, you should never doubt, even if your senses say, because doubt will ruin everything you have!"

5 THE YOGA OF TRUE RENUNCIATION

Arjuna got confused by understanding there is renunciation (declining) of actions and yoga of action, out of this which one to follow. Krishna told Arjuna, that Yoga through action is superior to waivering of action. The person who maintains evenness and neither hates nor desires and free from the pairs of opposites and performs unattached actions with no expectation on result is liberated. However renunciation is hard to obtain and only sages can do it. The one who is equipped with Yoga (evenness and unattached), his mind is pure, who has self conquered and mastered the senses, will not be tainted by actions. He understand that he doesn't perform anything, seeing, hearing, touching, smelling, eating, sleeping , letting go, catching hands, closing eyes and opening and everything , he offers to God. He lives like the lotus leaf with water, unattached. By body and by mind and by senses the yogis (one who follow Yoga) perform actions without attachment and

31

live in self-purification.

"Our Life: In our Life, we breathe and fill lungs, we pump the blood, we digest the food, we command the neural systems to work and unless we tell nothing of this will work.... Oh! Sorry! we do none of these activities, it's taken care by some power which is out of our normal thinking, but we believe if we eat, that's enough the body is taken care!!... Fact is we have a complete complex system as named "Body" of us, which is not in our control! (Do we ask the white cells to find and kill bacteria?) Nevertheless, the body acts with very high intellect and we are not aware of! Nevertheless whatever actions we do, we claim, it is done by us... For example, one day when we wake up, the arms are not working; can we command our arms to work? Not possible.... So when we aware that the micro system in our body is so well designed and till date and future also it's controlled by supreme power, why to claim the actions and the results .... The one who takes care of you and me, is taking care of that also, it all depends on him and all credit's/debit's goes to him and only him "

Krishna told Arjuna, the liberated one (yogin) treats a saint, a bird, a dog, a dog eater and every living being in the same way. He understands and sacrifices all the thinking and actions to me. He understands all the livings have birth and end, and he understands the bondage, relationship, attachment can bring him sorrow. Hence, he leaves everything to me and runs his life.

"Our Life: Many a times we separate the god from us and we believe that we are the doers. We keep god in a

corner of house/in room/in a cabin, we keep the god in temple/church/mosque, and we believe that god is only there. We think, in front of god, we should not do something, which is not auspicious. First, we have separated god from us, by design. Second, we think, we do all the things and god is only an invitee. Third, we believe god can only be there for good auspicious things and not for anything. Whereas god says, we need to give everything to him, and he says as a supreme power he is there everywhere and in every living being. However, we don't listen to him. Sometimes it is like, God owns a call centre, and we can ring whenever we want and we will raise a service request, and after some days, we will launch a complaint that he has not addressed the problem. Does not worry, many of us feel that we pay fee also for his service (monthly/yearly/etc)... "

6 THE YOGA OF SELF CONTROL

Krishna told Arjuna that a yogin is the one, who performs action without depending on the result, and not the one, who do not perform any action. The one who has won the thoughts can only reach yoga. The humans, should not lower themselves, and for a person who has self-conquered, his self-acts as friend. For the one who has not conquered the self, they see enemy in themselves. The yogin, who has conquered the self, for him the earth, sand, gold or anything, seems to be the same. The person understands there is nothing superior to him and nothing lower than him, and he concentrates on the supreme power.

"Our Life: In our professional and personal life, we see people behave differently with others, based on the position/achievement/status, others have obtained. When we speak to the CEO of organization, we think as if it is biggest achievement and when we speak to an office boy, we end up advising him or treating him as a poor

life. None of them is great or poor; they both are performing their own duty given in this world. An entrepreneur who employs 1000 people is not great and nor the person cleaning his office space is poor. It is a role given by the supreme power in this world. A person defeated continuously in his attempts, does not mean to be a loser in life, maybe he has better life without much attachments and has ability to handle failures. All the so-called great people had the ability to handle failures that is why they were great. When you sit in front of a top official in work place, do you need to be afraid or anxious? No. Whatever you know, whatever you perform, is required by the organization/industry/society that is the reason, you are employed, and so your role and action has to be acknowledged first by you. As an Individual, you might be much closer to the supreme power and you may have better understanding of life and work. So you don't need to be nervous and need not be aggressive, be a balanced person."

Krishna has explained Arjuna on how to perform physical yoga and concentrate, he also told, the one who sleeps and eats more or less, cannot practice them. A person, who sees the self, by self, and satisfied with it, will not have great sorrow. The person practicing yoga can concentrate on self and little by little he can remove the senses and attachments, anything that cause unsteadiness should be kept away. The person starts seeing me everywhere and in everything. For him, I never vanish. He who is having comparison with himself, sees everywhere me, he is highest yogi. Of all the yogis, the one who sees me in the inner self and merged in me, he according to me is the most devout.

"Our Life: There are three types of people , number one, person always looking at survival, for them life is all about living in that short period, anything they will do to survive. Number two, Comparative person, his life is always driven by the environment, social happenings and others. They just see others and try to compete and achieve results and again they start comparing. Number three, Leading person, for them in life there is no comparison, they want to lead/initiate something and they do it for themselves.

Most of us here are running a comparative life, and we do not want to look back our life. Fear... Yes we Fear! To know that, whether it is really a good life, what we are doing here, and so on... because we believe by the time, we think on this, others will cross us and go... so we keep pushing and compete with others... The leading person, mentioned here doesn't mean any top business person or some top official, they are those people who leads their way without any comparison in their mind and heart, they are not worried about anything new or change, because they have strong belief in themselves or supreme power. Either of these (Self belief or belief on Supreme power), according to god, is important for, to be a closer one to him."

7 THE YOGA OF WISE UNDERSTANDING

Krishna told Arjuna that he created Earth, water, fire, air, ether, mind, intellect and egoism and above all, he created the life itself. All this are woven on him, like a clusters of gems in a string. He went ahead and told, the taste of water, light of moon, syllable "Om" in Vedas, fragrance of earth, life in all, intelligence of the intelligent and radiance of the radiant, everything is being on him. The characteristics - Pure, active and inert are coming from supreme power, but he is not in them, these are divine illusions and very hard to overcome, only the one, who seek the supreme power will cross it. The distressed people, knowledge seeker, wealth seeker and wise man all worship him, out of these the wise man, who seek only him is dearer to him. I am in formless and in many forms as gods, people pray to different forms and want to achieve something and they go to achieve it. The one who believe in my supreme form reaches me and he is the unborn and imperishable. Krishna knows the past, present and future and him no one knows. The wise man at the time of departure (death) they pray to him and reach him, not only them, even the sinner who prays to him at the end realizing this, also reaches him.

"Our Life: The Universe is one amazing place and it has so many wonderful creations! However if you look at them closely, there is some pattern we can realize. The smallest components like cells in a body, atom in a metal and the biggest element the universe, all of them has a nucleus(centre) , free particles which move around , and well arranged particles like planet, electrons ,etc in a distance away, revolving around the nucleus in a orbit. Which shows, the base of all material elements and living beings have same commonality. Therefore, when we read, god is in there in everything, there is not much to surprise. Also as per Newton's law (yes... the school theory, which fetched easy marks!), the energy in this universe cannot be created and can't be destroyed, but it can only be converted to a different form. When it is a science theory, we don't ask question, the same when it comes in a holy book, we ask... God is unborn and imperishable and the same is for the soul, which are unborn and imperishable, but they can different forms with bodies... Science is nothing but a language used to study his creations, but science is neither the god nor it can lead us to god. Only belief can take us to the supreme power"

8 THE YOGA OF INDESTRUCTIBLE BRAHMA

Krishna explained to Arjuna, at the time of death/quitting the body, a person remembers the supreme personality of god as goal, then he achieves him, similarly he who meditates on Krishna and constantly engages himself in remembering the supreme personality of god- reaches him. Like that the one who reads Vedas and follows all the rules and guidance set by them also reaches him (if that's their goal), the same is for the one – who is dedicated his life in devotional service and completely followed that as a medium to reach. Beyond all these, the one who understand supreme personality, as oldest, as controller, as smallest, as largest, beyond material, beyond conception, seeing him as sun, moon and everything and live as yogin also reaches him.

Krishna has explained the practice of Yoga, on how to close eyes and think of the central point of in between eyes and thinking about god with the syllable of "Om" chanting, can help in achieving perfection. Similarly, he explained the calculation of days and nights for Brahma and for human, and he told - by period and day /night, when one can reach the birth less state. However, the one who firmly believes in supreme god and at the time of death, who only thinks on him, will reach Krishna – the supreme personality of God.

"Our Life: The very famous question, if tonight the world is going to be destroyed by a comet (think, NASA missed this) and there is no chance for USA, Russia or China to send their missiles to destroy it in the middle air, and it's official now, that you have only 2 hours with you..... What will you do...? Many of us would like to have our final wish fulfilled. Some in bars, some with family, some in roads, some in crying, some in phone, some in love, some with holy book & in church/temple/mosque, etc praying that it should not end today (basically asking god to do some magic to save them, so another few years they can lead their great life)... Not most of them are expected to be in a state of prayer which leads only to him and not thinking on anything else, instead many will be still searching for final set of happiness or pleasure or handling fear through pleasure or engage in action which makes them forget themselves. Interestingly not many of us are sure, whether instead of fulfilling materialistic or human desires, we will be realizing god!

The one who is studying the holy books or praying in holy place, they are still searching god outside in a paper (words) or in a place. There is nothing wrong in it. However, the moment you search god outside, the path is huge and it has no end. Many of them want to see god in a form or in an action, or in nature, or in a place... We think god has to come in front of us... Why should he come? .... God is inside you, if he is the super soul and has made all these souls, and all these souls are part of him, then your soul is the place where god resides... Do not search him outside... You may never find him! Let the moment be anything, he is there in you and he never leaves you... You be having tea, eating meat , helping someone, wounded, or working, let you do whatsoever, at every moment and at any time, he is there with you! We think only in a particular place he lives or he resides, that is nothing other than lack of awareness. He never leaves you alone, let it be success, failure, loss or anything, he is there with you and all your pain and pleasure he is taking. Be sure, you are part of him and there is nothing to worry, but you are not the god! Anyway, it's true not everyone can have the same understanding, so he has given many paths and religion and practices, so that based on understanding they can follow him (by doing devotional activity, meditate, pray, help others, etc)"

9 THE YOGA OF ROYAL SECRET

Krishna has told Arjuna, since he is the dearest and true disciple of supreme god, Krishna will tell the greatest secret to him. He told Arjuna, all the beings are part of him, but he is not completely in any one part. All beings here have a lifetime and at the end, they move out and come back again to this world. Some call this as nature, in which I send things repeatedly. Nor I am bound by any actions, but I keep doing the actions without any attachments. With my supervision the nature produces the moving and unmoving and the world revolves. I am the food, medicine, mantra, butter, fire, father of world, the mother, supporter and grandsire, I am the knowable, the purifier and syllable "Om" and all Vedas. I am the goal, sustainer, lord, witness, abode, shelter, friend, origin, dissolution, foundation, treasure and in many forms, and I am the imperishable. I give heat, cold, send rain, I am the immortal and I am the death and birth, existence and non-existence.

"Our Life: It's very difficult for us to accept all the happenings in life as part of god (not as act of god, but its part of god). This is primarily because the self is made of actions, desires and ego. A human loses the most and become weak, when he loses the loved one! Alternatively, the love itself! Why do we really get broke down that time, it is because we know, that we can never achieve it back... Nevertheless, why do we want to achieve it back? because we don't know what else to do, repeated memories which don't leave us, we don't see any replacement for that love, and our ego – which categorizes us as worthless, we are not ready to leave thinking, because we as a person feel it's wrong to forget.... Hmm... So many people lose their life, do suicide, put them off life, and do bad to their own... Why?, When god is everything and he lived/lives as your loved one and he is the one – who is dead or told you to forget or lost somewhere...if so, then why, we are carrying this sadness, for what we are waiting... When he (god) is gone from the form you loved, he will come in a new form, for you! There is nothing that you have lost! Whatever was there in some form and which you loved, will be there in some other form, but you have to be ready for that! Remember you will also die someday; you will also leave someone alone, someday! However, be sure, with them also god will be there! So accept the changes, as every change is also him... He is there for you, he never leaves you alone, and your loved ones will be there with him always, as Part of him... The only thing, which you can pray is, that they also should reach the supreme god and there is no return back to the world for them... So get up and walk, and never allow the

smoke surround you and make you feel lost"

Krishna told Arjuna about heaven and birth, the men who follow the Vedas, the soma drinker (holy drink), pure one, sacrifice and the worshipper; they all go to heaven and enjoy the divine pleasures of gods and demi gods. Once their merit is exhausted, they again enter in to this world as mortals. It is cycle in which going and returning happens to human, even if they follow all the Vedas. The men who worship me alone, for them I secure the place with me. Even the one, who worships any other gods or in any other forms, they only worship me. I am everything and the supreme power, the ignorant forget this. I am the enjoyer of all and the lord of sacrifice too, but when they do not know me, they fail. The worshipper of gods, go to that form; the ancestor's worshippers, goes to that form; the elements worshippers, go to that form; the one who worships me, comes to me. With devotion, if one offers a leaf, flower, fruit or water, I take that for their pure mind. Hence whatever you do or practice, do that as an offering to me. Thus, you shall be liberated from fruit's of action, good and bad. By thus, you shall come to me. I have none dear and none hateful, however the one who worship me with devotion, they are in me and I am in them. Even the sinful will reach me; by having, understand me and having devotion on me. So fix your mind on me, devote to me, and sacrifice to me, by this you shall reach me.

"Our Life: We might worship gods with many forms, but finally everything is one supreme power, this is told by god in Gita and not by us. So why do we have problems

here based on religion? What are we trying to do? Is god expecting us to conclude and bring justice to his land/principle/rules, etc? ... Ignorance, fear, politicizing, identity crisis and egoism, all of them is creating their own illusions to human mind, by thus we see people fight and safeguarding their gods... Yes... That is what we believe... We are the one, who safe guard our god and religion, by fighting with evil (all other forms, which we can't accept is evil for us...Krishna with any other name is also evil for us), if this is the belief we have means, then we should read Gita once again or many more times.... He is the supreme power and safeguarding everything. If someone really wants to perform their duty to their religion, then they should read and practice it... In addition, we become a fool, keep holy book aside, and fight with Krishna... Yes, by showing our grudge and hate on other religion, region or anything, we just showed it on Krishna and not on any other gods... (there is no other god, it's one supreme power , let it be Krishna, Allah, Jesus, Buddha or any).

Can anyone say that they safeguarded Bhagavad Gita? None can say that... on its own, it is surviving; it is just the wish of God. People can argue, unless they fought with other religions , it wouldn't have survived... check karnatic/Hindustani music, bharata natyam or any dance, none of them have well scripted manuals, but they survived for years, the same for few language and tradition...It's Just that, they are followed by people and that became part of their life.. When it comes to Bhagavad Gita or god, we will just fight, more than following . So then, why don't we understand and have fewer problems based on religion? May be, the supreme power wants to have balance between wise and ignorant…

As a secret, god has told that, offer everything to me and be detached from actions' fruitive result. It is easier, when we have poor result and we are ready to dedicate it to god, but when you get success, not many will offer it to god. The same is for fame! Success and fame, they both take you away from where you started, and no longer will you be detached, unless you dedicate it to god. We are seeing people, after success (like a writer, media person, movie maker, socialist, etc) they want to give comment on everything, they share their opinion on everything… very rarely, we see people who defy to comment and say they are not the right one to comment. We see newspapers are filled with additional pages, where people have to attend parties and they are rated. Does everyone feels happy for this, is that what the person is all about, may not be! However, Success and fame, takes you there, where coming back to ground is very difficult for you. The best way is, offer success, failure and everything to god and keep ourselves unattached to the results."

10 THE YOGA OF DIVINE GLORIES

Krishna continued and explained to Arjuna, that none of the rishis and forms of gods knows his origin! In addition, he is the source of all the Vedas, gods and rishis. The one, who understand Krishna as unborn and he is the source of all the worlds and lords, and live based on that, is liberated from sins and then enters in to birth less state. All the characteristics and happenings , intelligence, wisdom, truth, lie, pain, fear, death, birth, violence, non-violence, equanimity, fame, shame and everything arises from me. I create the great rishis (saints), demi gods and others in the universe. The one, who understand this glory of mine, will be able to establish in stable yoga. The wise understand this, and keep their thoughts on me, they are dedicated to me and they enlighten others and they always speak about me, and they get delighted and devout, thereby with yoga they come to me. I reside in their self, remove the ignorance, give them the wisdom, and take them with me.

"Our life: The supreme power is not an equation or a formula to understand and to apply logic. Before Einstein derived the formula E= MC Power 2, the world was not aware of that, and people might had laughs! Today, if I show you a Computer motherboard circuit and ask you to explain or I show you a design of a Dam Structure and ask you to explain, you may not be able to do! Why, because we need to study and understand that, then we will be able to interpret! For a small chip and paper of design , if we need to study 4 to 5 years to understand, then the creator of universe and creator of all living beings and non-living beings, can he be understood in days, months, or year? Then why to make fun or make others to disbelief, which we are not aware of! On the other side, is that meaning, you need years and years to reach him? No, you need months, or week, or a day, or even a minute, or less than a second to reach him... Because, he never leaves you alone, he is there within you. The solution for all complex things comes from your mind... Ask and search your mind to get those answers... Your mind has all the secrets, inventions and answers, in built ... just search and take it... I don't think Google or any search engines can help, but determination and belief is the clue for that search!"

Arjuna requested Krishna to tell more on the supreme god's glories and he is eager to listen. Then Krishna spoke, Of the rishis – I am Narada, I am the beginning-middle-end, I am life on all beings, I am the sun, moon and Vishnu, of Vedas- I am sama, of senses – I am mind, of rudras- I am sankara, of mountain – I am meru, of generals – I am skanda, of offerings – I am prayer, of men- I am the king, of weapon- I am thunderbolt (vajra), of serpents – I am vasuki, I am varuna (god of rain), I am yama(god of death), I am wind, I am shark, I am ganges, I am the knowledge of self, I am the beginning letter "A" , I am the death, I am the fortune, I am memory, I am month, I am flower, I am cheat, I am gambler, I am effort, I am goodness, I am badness, I am punishment, I am silence, I am the knowledge, I am the seed, I am the moving and I am non-moving and there is no end to my divine glories. I just gave you few examples, but all the existence and non-existence only comes from me. This world and universe is one part of me, but I am not a complete part in anything. Again, I am unattached to anything and I am performing my duty.

"Our Life: In our day to day life, we never realizes, what are we? Where our life is going? Who controls us? And so on... We never ask any questions, about us and why we are part of this world... We feel uncomfortable to ask such questions....Because we know those answers, will bring some level of detachment to things, with which we have attachment, also the fear of losing the race with others. There are many of us, who think, why should I ask such question? I am happy with my life and I have children, I have assets, etc, then why I need to be bother what's what?!!.. In addition, we believe that spending time in these questions is meaningless. I agree to you, if your aim is not to understand and reach the supreme god, but to gain some good deeds and spend life as it is, like ant/tiger/monkey/wolf/plant/bird or like any other

living being, then you are perfectly right. You will also lead a life, which is prefixed; you will also have happiness, sadness, success, failure and everything, like the one who follows the supreme god's path. The difference will be, the one who understand the glory of supreme power will not get un-equanimity and will not be stressed by the happenings at any time, but you will! Anyways, not everyone is born to follow the path told by supreme god, if so, then there will no balance in the life systems here, because everyone might reach- no birth state! We all learnt that earth is revolving at high speed, but we never feel that movement, similarly still, we think that sun "rises" and "sets", that is what we are! It needs determination and belief to realize god, without that, we will lead a life, in which "we" do everything only! Moreover, we can proudly say, "Ignorance is bless".

However for the one, who understands the supreme personality of god is everything, his expectation in life, with people, with activities, with relationship and with everything is absolute, but he performs his duty and he realizes the god in himself!

To reach such a mindset, for some it is easy, for some it needs constant practice. The mind is practice oriented for most of its part! If you keep watching/reading crime movies for a year, you will be able to simulate any place as a crime scene place! If you see religion based channels, you keep talking about them; it is same for fashion, education, agriculture, health, food, travel, etc... The mind can easily be cheated and manipulated and it easily takes the wrong one! Hence, for some people, practice or constant engagement is required to be there in yogic condition, but it's not for all! "

11 THE YOGA OF COSMIC FORM

Brief Expectation Setting:

Before we read this chapter, it is important for us to be imaginative. So, we will now imagine "Sun" in our mind... take few seconds... ok... How big was the sun we imagined? a paper size or a building size or mountain size ... our imagination was nothing but, how we see the sun in normal life, it's something far away and looks like a car wheel size ... But the fact is , Sun is more than a million times bigger than what you imagined... now try to magnify the size by 100 times.. Then by 1000 times... Then to a million times... oops... the memory is fully dumped, brain is unable to process the image... now you might feel like restarting your brain! See, this is the power of imagination and truth...but we like to live with our own illusions... coming back, this imagination to an extent is required to experience this chapter...

Chapter for Dummies:

Arjuna told Krishna, that his illusions are gone, and he realized Krishna is everything, and having known that, he is now interested in seeing god in all those forms, which god has prescribed. He asked Krishna is that possible for him to see that form? Krishna told, the divine form has many a million sorts of things in it, with varied colors and shapes, and many more gods and living beings and everything is there in it, and no one, has ever seen that before. Krishna told, whatever Arjuna wants to see, everything, irrespective of time, geography, secrets, and forms, he can see them all. Krishna told Arjuna, for him to see such a form a divine eye is required and he blessed him with that. Then the god has shown the universal and timeless form to Arjuna.

"Our Life: I had this question, that why a special eye do is required, can't we see in our normal eye that form... Hmm... When I go to a 3d movie, unless I wear a special glass, I don't see anything there, in fact the picture is more blur, the moment I wear the glass, I can feel 3d... When I see picture in picture Television, I am not able to recognize all the happenings in the nine screens in a moment of time in my mind, though the television might show everything. Similarly, my eyes can cover nearly 180-degree vision, but unless I concentrate not all the happenings in that visible area is recognized by mind... My eyes can't see something in dark, but a special binocular is able to see... so many things, my eyes can't do, even though this is the best intelligent automatic focus lens in the world, ever produced. Now I realize why Arjuna needed a special divine eye for this..."

The universal form has contained many mouths and eyes, divine ornaments everywhere, and holy weapons held in thousands of hands, wearing divine garlands and colorful rays of light everywhere and it's like thousands of suns have joined together in one place, there are faces everywhere. Arjuna was seeing more and more in that form and started speaking to the Supreme god, I see all the gods in you, all the saints in you, I see thousands of faces, and so many arms, stomachs, and I don't see there is any beginning, middle and end to this form, there is no dimension and angle which I can quote, it's spread across everywhere, there are wonderful lights, flowers everywhere spanning, the Vedas produced, it's difficult to take all of this. I see the sun, moon and all planets in some portion of your this body, I see face of fire, water, air which sends them in to this world, the heaven and earth is inside you, the form is marvelous and at the same time terrible. I see the saints praying, I see the demons killing, and I see the soldiers, animals, workers, birds, serpents, good deeds, bad deeds and all coming from you from many of your mouths. I see my relatives crushed in to your mouth, I see the good and bad people undergo different treatments, I see the souls separated and go into a mouth and new birth happens to them in another mouth. I see the past of the entire world, I see the future of this entire world, I see fiery faces of yours, which destroys the living beings, and by looking all of this I am terrified.

"Our Life: That Arjuna was none other than me and you, he has seen the universal form of god and he is unable to bear it. Important question is that more than Full HD quality or may be better than that? Definitely it will be better than that, because it was not a telecast to decode it, the eyes were taking that vision as it is ... (unless we

have negative power in our eyes, if so, then use some disposable HD lens:)). What is that universal form for me now, it's more than watching a Disney pictures movie or Avatar movie, the lights are so colorful spanning beyond sky to beneath earth, the god was having thousands of faces each with different color, skin tone, action, shape, etc , we can see Atlantic ocean to Pacific ocean in a mouth of one face, Himalayas to alps all mountains in one face, Arctic snow in a face, Sahara to Kalahari desserts in one face, all the nuclear ammunitions in one face, all the volcano's in one face, like that so many... we can see all 500 crore people's life at one instance, we can see all their past, we can see all their future, we can see all the animals individually and their past and present, similarly we see all the plants, we see underneath layers of world, we see all the planets in this universe, we see beyond milky way what is there!, We see Jesus, Nabhi, Vishnu, Buddha , Greek gods and the holy faces and we see the wordings of all the holy books in one moment ! not only that, We see the Swiss bank accounts and secret numbers of all the billionaire, We see the future of earth's future, we see the past of this world for many million years in a second, we see the colors we can never recognize, we see the millions of cows, we see millions of Bacteria, we see the all the scams in the world at one moment, we see all the violence in one moment, we see all the poor searching for food, we see all the riches making the money die to store in their graveyard cupboards, we see all the share markets sliding, we see all the pollution coming from the motor vehicle at a moment, we see our parents birth and death, we see our children birth and death and we see *our self born and die....if you imagined this well, you would have exhausted by this time ! Hydrate yourself please!"*

Arjuna was telling Krishna, having seen such faces of god, fire, killings, destruction and recreations from you, I am really becoming unrest and I have no peace with me. All the great warriors and my forefathers are getting destroyed and they get in to you and some undergo real bad treatment in this process, as all the rivers goes in to sea- I see all of the famous, heroic people also goes into your mouth in a hurry for their destruction, and I see fiery race everywhere. I have seen these fiery forms of in you, who you are with these forms, he asked Krishna. Supreme god replied, I am the destruction and time, I engage in destructing the world and its living and non-living beings in every moment. He also told, even without Arjuna gets in to the battle, the Kauravas and their supporters will be destroyed, and Arjuna is only a tool for this action. Arjuna is not the one who actually kills, it is Krishna who already killed them and it's going to happen in a moment. Arjuna bowed in front of god and told, now I understand why everyone praise you and saints pray to you, you are the imperishable, all the planets and everything comes from you, I bend in front you with my devotion as offering. I addressed you in my life differently in different time, treating you very normally, in the process I would have insulted you some time, please forgive me, you are the father of world, you are greatest guru in this world, I understand you are the supreme. I am delighted as I see the form, which no one ever seen; now I want to see you in the divine peaceful form with four arms, to get peace to my mind. Please provide such a view of yours to me. Krishna told you have seen the universal and supreme form of mine, this is my original form, none has seen it before, not by any rituals, austerities- one can see this form and none other than you can see this form, now do not be afraid and get confused, I return to the form, which you requested. Then god has shown the four-armed universal form to Arjuna.

"Our Life: When we see a man, who is seven feet tall (172" inch) and with broad shoulder around 46" inch and when he crosses us, there is some nervousness we get! When we sit in front of a sea, its nice experience, now if we see some big waves come from it, we catch nervousness! We travel on road, suddenly a huge noise, and two vehicles had accident, and we see people with blood, again some nervousness! If that is what we are, then suddenly we see god who is not measurable in height ... (oh! human need some measurement to imagine, else it is difficult... so take for example more than 2000 meters/6000 feet ++++) and that to with so many hands and heads, how do we feel? Think the closest person in your life, the person's work is now changed and daily that person needs to kill minimum 2 people and then they will meet you... How would you feel about the person, with this activity? So when god, who according to us, is always pleasant and do only favorable things to us (we need him for doing favors :)), suddenly shows the destructing side of him, do we feel normal... No way, we might need lemon juice, some ice pack and someone to say "All is Well" :)... in

this entire process, what we understand is that we also imagined the universal form to an extend we can! This imagination power is nothing but his blessing alone, without him the power to imagination will not there! The Arjuna was none other than you and me, the god has shown the universal form, in our mind. Having seen such a form of him, now it's time for you to see the form of a cool four armed universal form... hope we can still imagine, so I leave it to you!.. Don't worry in most of our life, we live with imagination only, without imagination- solutions, resolute, creation, destruction and nothing will born! In fact, imagination is a blessing given by god! (What will happen, if I get up one day in the morning, and I realize the entire life, which I lived was my one-day dream!) "

12 THE YOGA OF DEVOTION

Knowing the supreme god, Arjuna wanted to know which is the best way to reach him and what kind of people are dearer to the supreme god. Krishna told Arjuna, the one who always worship me with faith and keep their mind in me is perfect, and the others who control the senses and do welfare to others reach me. Krishna told there are various ways of reaching him, by fixing the mind on Krishna and engaging all the intelligence on Krishna, the person lives within Krishna, however if that's not possible, then involve in meditational practices to attain the supreme power, if that's not possible, then should involve in devotional service, if that's not possible, then give all your results of action to me and work, if that's not possible, work on developing knowledge on me.

"Our Life: At least In India we see, people worshiping god in numerous forms, from stone to animal to human to giant humans, etc. These forms are

made to believe god is in every form and few of the practices are made to regularize the people's engagement in devotional activities, like a month long festival, a month long prayer, etc. They tend to change the nature of people by this consistent practice. In addition, the forms of gods are mostly family based like son, mother, etc. They help people understand how they need to live in their life and gods are more like super models (in family life). As we go to an ashram or Matt we understand that people learn Veda's and they perform rituals, etc ...In places like Himalayas we could see yogis, who has no desire and perform no action to live, who live mostly in mediation... People like us , who love to hear about god , what it is , why it is and try to argue few things, it's nothing but we try to develop knowledge in that area (and some goes to religious meeting and prayers to learn on this).. Some people believe helping others and performing good things is the service to god... All of them are path to reach the supreme power, however at any point in time, if you think, by doing this you will definitely reach god; you already lost your path!

We see advertisement boards on donated products, we see names of people kept for charity trust, we see temples built on every street/community - it seems god should serve their street/community also, we see that rituals overtake underlying principles told in Gita, we see people go to religious meetings to develop contacts and feel proud to organize such meetings in their place and so on.... by doing all this, we already lost our path to reach him and again his illusions are hard to come by! (We are proving by doing all this)"

Krishna told to Arjuna, the one who is not envious but friendly to all living beings, free from false ego, who is always satisfied, who is tolerant, who is self-controlled, whose mind and intelligence is fixed on me, such a person is very dear to me. One who neither rejoices nor grieves, who waivers the auspicious and inauspicious things, who is equipoise in honor and dishonor, fame and infamy, who is fixed in knowledge and who is engaged in devotional service, such a person is very dear to me. Those who follow devotional service path and who are completely engages themselves with faith and making me as supreme goal is very dear to me.

"Our Life: Can we be not envy about what happens with our friends and relatives like promotion, marriage, assets, etc? Sure we can... first thing we have to acknowledge and respect ourselves and our life, second thing we have to understand there is nothing more than the supreme personality of god , and all others have no value... So then why did I say, first you need to respect your self... it's because the supreme personality of god lives in you, that's why you need to first respect yourself.

Ego is a very important emotion for a human being, beyond a point it can make you like an animal. Ego basically comes from comparative nature of us, either to prove to someone or to society or group of people - that we are not inferior or to prove we are superior...People want to go on VIP lane in some places, if no permission is given, then their ego is triggered, people don't want to

follow certain rules, but when they are forced, their ego is triggered, people want to have last word in any discussion, if not, then ego is triggered and so on.... The person who is not self-aware and who can be taken by the situation for a ride, will undergo this for many times... False Ego, can create emotional imbalance, which means meaningless speech and activity to follow, and will take you in to trouble. Finally, to resolve this, you have to either tell lie or imagine yourself that others has done very wrong things to you (may be more than what was the reality)... To overcome the False Ego, it is very important to realize yourself, see god in others, believe in the actions of god and do not attach you for fame and honor. Because when you are attached to something, false ego can be easily triggered. We are sure in most of the violence and relationship breaking; false ego is the main cause. By losing this characteristics, you will have better life (as your relatives/friends/known or anyone whom you interact will be also comfortable). However, it does not mean being a fool or allow others to dominate you... Be firm when it is right and it is your duty, but never be egoistic!
"

13 THE YOGA OF THE FIELD AND IT'S KNOWER

Arjuna asked Krishna to explain what is field, what knower of field is, what knowledge is, what nature is and what is living being in it. Krishna explained to Arjuna, the body of the self is called Field, the person who understand his body and its senses, is called person who knows the field. The understanding of them is knowledge. The body has five great elements, egoism, intellect, ten senses and mind, desire, hatred, pleasure, pain, intelligence, fear, etc and when they combine with mind, they derive all the actions... The humility, modesty, forgiveness, service to teacher, purity, steadiness, self control, absence of attachment to objects, absence of egoism, Clarity in perception of birth- death-old age-sickness and pain, unattached to affection of son, wife, home and maintaining equality for desirable and undesirable, constant in self realization, all of them are called knowledge. The things, which are opposite to this, are ignorance. The one who understand his body and separate himself with his knowledge is the one, who reaches me.

"Our Life: Have you noticed; wherever you find a mirror, irrespective of how many times we have seen ourselves in a day, many of us like to see once again in the mirror! Check when you are in office washroom, restaurant, hospital, shopping market, anywhere... If we take a stock that how much time we spend time in gratifying the bodily senses, it might be very interesting information for us... We spend lot of time in external care of the body, the look, the color, skin care, hair growth and so on (good for cosmetics seller) then we spend time in satisfying the taste senses , search for food, restaurants, snacks and then physical and mental satisfaction on through various activities.. Most of us live for the sake of satisfying the body and its senses and nothing more for us... Do we ever try to distinguish the body and our self separately? Very rare...so when a pain comes to your body, it heavily affects your mind and senses, because you have always given your body the priority... When your senses are not satisfied, you get wild, your mind goes out of control (example: if you do not have tasty food for few days, are not you get wild with family member or service provider?)... Some people have low confidence, because physically they do not appear great, whose mistake is this! It is only theirs... Knowledge is superior, and our mind should constantly work on it, then our body and its senses take less priority, so that we can control"

Krishna told Arjuna, the supreme power is in every being, it's smaller and larger, it's undivided but yet divided, it's unmoving but yet moving, it's the light and also darkness, the understanding of these phenomenon is knowledge. The nature has all the materialistic things span across and that's the cause, the living being with their characters like desire, ego, attachment, senses they utilize the nature and produce actions, which will result in good/bad, pleasure/pain, etc. I am the lord as a spectator, a permitter, an enjoyer and a non-enjoyer; I keep performing my duties without any attachments. The one who understand these, and performs the action, will never born again. The one can see supreme lord in all beings, he never destroys the self, because of this virtue, and he reaches god. A man who understands that all desires and actions are of this nature and senses, he will attain the supreme god. The one, who can understand, the body, knowledge of body, nature and living being characteristics, will be able to cross over and reach the supreme god.

"Our Life: We develop our knowledge based on the question "Why", and we understand the logic in the answer and we gain our knowledge. From childhood, this is the technique we follow to gain our knowledge. Hence most of the time, we need some logic which we can understand, to qualify an information as knowledge and store in our mind and work accordingly. However not always we need logic to satisfy ourselves and act, this is very much true when there is high negative or positive benefit is involved. In that case, we accept anything without logic. While walking in a street,

someone says, in Next Street there is a street pump which flows lava (volcano eruption) in to the street and many of them injured, we will not even go there... Though we may know, there is no possibility of that... Even when someone said, the gods' idol is drinking milk, we all carried milk... When someone takes away gods' idol from his mouth, we all see that as god's blessing...This very nature of us, runs in the mind and controls the senses. When someone says, don't think about a monkey, we think about it... why, because we want to know why? If they say to you, the moment you think about monkey, you will die...again you will think... It is because fear! ... Fear of change/impact is a major reason to think adversely...Why we have fear. Because we like the current position of us and we do not want change from it...more than that we are attached to the elements, body, relationship, etc... so we don't want change, so fear creeps in, when fear is there - we don't need logic, our knowledge breaks... in that situation, we can act as ill, superstitious, cry and lower our stability. So we have to keep using the question "why", but when we do not use it, it means there is something that we need to take care of it... At the same time, we take little information about a logic (which we can understand) and we store them as knowledge. (Fire will burn! we do not test it, we just take this information as knowledge)... Therefore, the knowledge has to be complete even about our body, attachments, senses and everything... If we do not have it, then senses (like fear, happiness, etc) will start controlling us, which leads only to misery.

God's creations and he himself is an Oxymoron or

conflicting thing.... unless we understand him, this would be our view point. The smallest atom, when split can destroy a country! The lightest air can uproot any structure! The smallest of a cell, can create a human! And so on, how the sky is clear and visible at a distance, but when you reach there, there is no end to it, that is how god also! He has no end and no beginning and he is the smallest but the largest, he kept the secrets and knowledge of all secrets in our mind also and in the universe also! Like water, he fits in the form you want! It is up to us to think in the way we want! You think him as a flower; he comes to you as flower! You think him as knife; he comes to you as knife! So it's up to us (by the way, when I say us, it includes him also, without him, there is no you, I and us!)"

14 THE YOGA OF THE THREE GUNAS

Krishna told Arjuna that he is the seed-giving father of all living beings and the form of body of all living beings. As living beings are born, by the very nature, they get three gunas (Characteristics), namely goodness (Sattva), Passion (Rajas) and Ignorance/Darkness (Tamas). Every living being consists of these three gunas. The goodness consists of knowledge, wisdom and illumination, the Passion consists of desire, pleasure, pain, attachment, etc and the ignorance consists of darkness, madness, cruelty. The Goodness in a person can overrule passion and ignorance, similarly passion can overrule the goodness and ignorance, similarly Ignorance can overrule the goodness and passion, all of these happening at any instance in a living being life and over a period. At the time of death if one mainly consists of Goodness (over a period of time), then he reaches the heaven and he is born again in between good rational people, if one consists of passion then he takes birth again, in between greedy action oriented people and the one consists of Ignorance goes to hell and born again with the similar people or as animal. The one who understand all these three characteristics actually drives the living being, and when he realizes it's only the supreme god who is creating the illusion, will stay away from them, by not attaching himself with action and it's result, he will not hate happiness or sadness as both are same for him, and this person reaches the supreme god.

"Our Life: Let us put few questions before us, is there any time we helped to the one who deserved? Is there any time we felt happy and thought, why does not the time stops at this instance or I can die at this instance? Is there any time really we felt cheated or betrayed or we tried to give an unwanted feedback on someone? Truly, for most of us, the answer will be yes, it is nothing but we travel across the goodness, passion and ignorance characteristics. When we help, if we understand the person's condition is improved with that help, it's goodness, however if you feel happy for that, maybe we are entering in to Passion, and if we feel only we can do that then we are ignorant. In a simple action, these three characteristics can dominate a person. Most of us live in Passion as the dominant character for us, because that drives us to do actions and makes us feel happy, sense of achievement, etc... At the same time we become emotional, sensitive, bring misery, etc... In an Indian common man life , he spends most of his time in talking on politics, cricket(sports), movies and actors, share market and land and then new addition is spirituality with meditation (or health) for some

men/women it's extended fashion and food & travel. All of these are passion for us, we talk, we see, we read on all these and satisfy our mind and sense, which is purely driven by the passion. More than spending times on self-realization... leave it... We cannot sit quite for an hour, without television, mobile, radio, or people... We always need someone/something to satisfy or interact; this is where Passion drives us mainly. If someone praises our action, our achievement, or us we are not happy. Yes, most of us like it... If someone comes and gifts you a wrapped box, are not we curious to open and see...Some of the also calculate the worth of the gift, based on what we gifted for that person and we expect similar or high return :)... Sometimes we are happy, when the who never listened to us get punished/facing problems and then we like say to him, see I told you... sometimes we go and aggressively pray to god, that the other person should get good punishment for the activity he has done... some of us, also challenge the other person, that we will teach them a lesson... Who are we? What do we think we are doing? Good or bad it comes to a person as they act, if someone deserves they will get... but we cannot dump our mind with ignorance and darkness, just by showing vengeance... Yes,... it is difficult to practice... However the more we restraint ourselves in teaching lessons to others or asking god to go and do action for us, the better it's for our mind... Believe no one can go out of the rule here.... whatever we think that some are enjoying their life , though they don't deserve it... believe their life is nothing but full of misery and they live in ignorance....

The life here is not measured by the wealth you have or caste you are born or position you are in... It's only measured by how close you are with the supreme personality...truly, there shouldn't be any gap between us and him, because we are him and he is Us.... so what do we need here more! And what life could be better than this?..."

15 THE YOGA OF SUPREME BEING

Krishna told Arjuna that the Vedas talk about a banyan tree, which is upside down, where the roots are grown up and the branches are coming down, the upper part of roots are the Vedas and the branches are the three characteristics (Gunas) and the roots which are growing downward reaches the human society, none of the people are aware it's start and end, but one has to understand that they have to cut the branches of these tree with the weapon called detachment to reach the supreme god. Krishna went ahead and told, All the living entities in the world are my parts, due to the senses and the characteristics they lead a life in a conception and based on that life, they carry the aroma (with the soul) and enters in to the new body. With the new body, the soul attains a new form of ears, eye, tongue, nose and senses, etc. Based on the new senses and mind the body again performs action. The ignorant will not understand his current life, his body and the characteristics he has, nor can he understand how his soul can reach a new body. However, the one who is in self-realization can see this clearly. The splendor of sun, moon and fire comes from me, I enter in each planet, I keep them in orbit, I am the fire of digestion, I am the air of life, I nourish the plants and I am seated in everyone's heart and from me comes remembrance, forgetfulness and everything. All Vedas know me, I am the Vedas and I am the knower of the Vedas. The perishable material world and imperishable spiritual world everything comes from me and I am the Supreme Being and called supreme soul, who is beyond all this. The one, who knows this and lives within me, will have no birth.

"Our Life: When I read this, I noticed that the new body with new ears, eye, tongue, etc is born based on the previous life, here the wonderful thing is there is no similarity between them. The fingerprints of 500+ crore people are different, and the previous generation of 400+ crore people were different and it's the same for all the previous generation. In fact, this is the true unique id every human is having! Same is for the eye pupil. Why can't they be the same, even at least randomly, why they never the same? How such a unique design is possible, though with bare eye, they all look same within that 1.5* 1.5 cm thumb... Similarly, we say 7 people look same in the world, at least till now we haven't seen anyone in the same way, even the twins born with certain difference. Who is the creator or designer for this? Do not worry about cloning, that is still done from using same cells of a person...it's a Xerox technique...

Similarly, we all read Darwin's rule about evolution, and I personally like it and believe it. What I like about it, is the relationship it has brought about on the nearby species in a table. However, it doesn't say that the evolution's happened without any supreme power...it can't also... in every period of world the god has taken different forms and different kind of animals where there and even human may not exist also in there... In last 2000 years at least we have our history is clear, but we have not seen any evolution, we never heard a new type of animal is born, even for that matter at least for last 5000 years we are sure..If it's just because of evolution, we would have expected modified human being, but I guess we are the same... (Don't count the result of fast food on human being :))... However yes, we see lot of new germs is coming... may be the demons are no longer with multiple arms; they have become bacteria, virus and nuclear weapons...

What does this mean to us is nothing but a supreme personality, which creates and maintains the system and living beings. It has complete control on all the living beings on this world and their life. It creates and destroys or resets the entire world and new set of species are born! However for us our running is important in life, and comparison is important in our life, and making fun of others is important in our life, whereas we have no clue that we ourselves is completely controlled by the supreme power and not only we , but the entire world. We do this, because we always think that supreme power is somewhere outside of us and for our life we need to run! Yes... We need to do the duties but without attachments and we can also realize the supreme personality within us"

16 THE YOGA OF DIVINE AND DEMONIC

Krishna told Arjuna, there are two kind of nature available, one is divine and another is demonic. The divine nature is purity, fearless, steadiness, self-knowing, austerity, truth, non-violence, absence of anger, modesty, forgiveness, energy, absence of pride, etc...The demonic nature is anger, ignorance, self praising, no purity, no truth, no good conduct, live for that moment and ready to sacrifice things for their happiness, small intellect, pride, arrogance, cruel desires, delusion, sensual enjoyment is the highest aim, wrath, grieving, unjust means, wealth accumulation for sensual enjoyment, believing that today is gained by them, hold everything, desire to hold all wealth for future, believing they change life, they manage people, they can do harm, they are the successful one and even believing they are strong and their health is managed by them. The demonic nature brings ego, greed, pride, false sacrifices, delusion and addiction towards habit's, sense gratification, self-honoring, stubbornness, power misuse, etc. The people who are with this nature, they even hate god and they cannot see me in their own bodies or in others. These evil doers will born in between demons only. By their act, these demonic nature people never reach me. Greed, anger and strong sexual desire these three should be avoided, to come out of demonic nature. A person, who comes of these three gates of darkness, can do well to self and to others and he will reach me. The person, who neglects these, will not be able to come across the darkness and can never attain perfection and happiness not the supreme goal.

"Our Life: Let's think for a minute and find out three activities for which we are proud of ourselves... count 1 to 60 if we want... now, if we had even one activity for which proud of in our life, then we yet to understand Gita. There is nothing for us to be proud of ourselves, they all come from one supreme soul, nor we have to feel that we are bad...The Divine and Demonic nature, these may not be exclusively available in a human, it can be in a mix. How many times we have seen that position, money, power/authority brings in easily the greed, misuse, and pride to people and they lose themselves in this nature. A security guard can get arrogance by his authority , an officer gets it and politician gets it, and you and me would have unknowingly used the authority we have , as a tool to satisfy our mind and senses! We have to consciously separate them from us, from the self! When we go to a temple/church/ people rush in front of

god, hit each other and try touch a place/idol/get some sacred products/etc... What purpose? A temple/mosque /church is a place for peaceful worship , but wherein the places have become revenue centers and people forget the peace and fight with each other to do their rituals/duty (for us, going to holy places have become duty, rather than feeling the supreme power there :)) .. Are these activities are Divine or Demonic? Well we know the answer... In our life, if every one of us tries to see what we are doing, we all can realize that we too have the demonic nature... Constantly and consciously, we need to cut them... With whom we spent maximum time in our life we spent, according to us? ... a) Wife b) mother c) friend or d) child. Answer is none of the above, It is SELF. If we have such demonic characters, it means that we are the first enemy to ourselves; we ruin our life and why to blame others... By changing us and looking at the supreme goal, the maximum time we spent being in divine nature....

This is at not only personal level, but also think about countries and the rulers; the power also gives them demonic nature. The countries and borders are nothing but logical division of land to preserve certain rules, tradition and for better management. The borders which exist now, where not there 200 years before, the border which was there 600 years before is not there now, the one in future may be completely different. People bring in patriotism to ensure, traditions are kept safe and to have better management, but over a period, the humanity is dead, now the borders have become cause of concern for humanity... People think the person beyond this line or fence is my enemy... what have the world thought to humanity? Grudge, vengeance, terrorism, racism, no acceptance, etc... Every country spends huge money to safeguard their borders and let their soldiers die, for nothing but a logical division of land... because every country believes that others will demolish the identity of their country, everybody spends... in this process, every country things that others are cheats, crooked, etc... So by design, this is how we start to see a foreign country and a foreigner, so humanity is gone. Beyond this, the countries which are rich and powerful, they are greedy enough to hold wealth and destabilize and control (demonic nature plays) and in return, they get wrath from other countries... Maldives is the first country which will be submerged under the sea, so the people are migrating to different countries... So what is a country here mean for them? It's piece of land, where they live... If in America, huge cyclones forms on weekly basis or heavy earthquakes rocks on daily basis, even those people have to move out of the great America... Therefore, what is a country here means...nothing but a logical division for cultural/traditional and management purpose... So why to have demonic nature, just for the land, which is anyway governed by the supreme power..."

17 THE YOGA OF THREE FOLD FAITH

Arjuna asked Krishna, how the faith is situated in people who have the characteristics of goodness (Sattva), Passion (Rajas) and Ignorance (Tamas). Krishna told Arjuna, that threefold faith depends upon the character, which they carry. The human becomes of the same as his faith. The men who punish their body in the name austerity and do not feed and make their body suffer, are fools, as they do not care that I am inside them. The men who eat, juicy and leafy foods can carry the goodness characteristics, the men who eat, too sour, spicy, salty food will carry passion characteristics and the one who eat stale, tasteless and impure food will carry Ignorance characteristics with them. The one who is in goodness, do the worship and offering without any expectations, and the one in Passion, provide offerings with expectations and meeting goals, and the one in ignorance, provide offering without any faith, but as to achieve immoral things. The Austerity of body is achieved by worshiping god, purity, Straightforwardness and taking care of health. Austerity of Speech is achieved by speaking pleasant and beneficial, and speaking truth. Austerity of mind is achieved by self-control, silence, purity in thinking. Beyond this any austerity which is practiced with object of getting reward, result, and honor will be of nature passion, which is unstable. The Austerity that is followed foolishly is set to be ignorance. When a charity is performed, that has to be without any result to achieve and for worthy person, then it is goodness. The same for a result if it is performed then it's for passion, the same performed for honor, and for unworthy person then it's ignorance. For the one who performs charity, austerity and others, only with faith on supreme power and with no other goal to achieve, he achieves all the three-fold faith.

"Our Life: In our day to day life, we see television, read newspaper, travel across so many advertisement hoardings and shops, but we don't notice all of them. The moment, we decide that we will buy two wheeler or four wheeler, house, etc... We are able to see number of advertisement in the same newspaper, television channel and in shopping places.... Are they published as per our wish...? No... They always exist, only thing, we do not notice them... The moment we started searching, we are able to see them (one exception, now a day's media team also searches only hot topics, and once rating goes down, they go to next topic!)... So search with faith, we will get what we want... For god, why do we need to search...? He is there in you, but faith is required...Belief

is required... You need to believe that he is there within you.... there is only one language and one short road to the supreme power , that's nothing but belief on him.... We swallow and excel air, do we stop this process? No, if we stop this, we will die... What is air? Is this not part of supreme power, our body is not of supreme power? Everything is from him... Then why do we believe that he is only in Pooja room, in a photo, or in a place... Are we thinking, he is a genie from Aladdin lamp, that whenever I hit, god will come out? :) .. Similarly, we have many rituals, and I strongly believe some of them have scientific reasons and cleanliness is associated with it, beyond that there is nothing... When we have death in house, birth in house, the woman in menstrual period, and so on, we treat them as inauspicious.... if god is there in graveyard (ex: Shiva), god is there in a woman's body and soul and god created the wonderful birth , then it's foolish to differentiate god from all of this.. Is he visitor to your house to come and eat food/Prasad and to go? He is the supreme power, without him nothing exists in this world even for a second... He is the blood, he is the air, he is the water, he is life, he is material and everything... Consider cleanliness, but never think god is not there in anything... Whatever we perform we give everything to god, beyond that if we try to treat him as angry young man/ angry bird or killer or money lender or sacrificer or leader or in any other form, he will come to us only in that form.... Not everyone can follow the systems with understanding, so based on people's capability the rituals are created and over a period of time and place and kind of people they have become rules... However if you believe he is a light, he is the light for you... If you imagine, he is a gun, he will be a gun for you...Because he has no attachment and he is equal to everyone...It's our faith which leads to what we deserve..."

18 THE YOGA OF MOKSHA BY RENUNCIATION

Arjuna asked Krishna, what is sacrifice and what is sannyasa (living as saint) in terms of action. Krishna told Arjuna, declining all the actions to satisfy material nature, leads to sannyasa, surrendering the fruitive results leads to sacrifice. At any time, worshiping, sacrifice and charity should not be given up; this even helps the purest souls to achieve higher state. However if they are performed with attachment, then they are of no use. When the prescribed duties are performed without expectation of result then it is of goodness, the prescribed duties are selectively performed and with expectations then it is of passion, the duties declined because of illusion then it is of ignorance. It is impossible for someone to be without any duties; hence leaving the results to me is the best. The body, performer, senses, undertakings and super soul all of them combined perform action, so if anyone think that he also did the action, it means he is ignorant. In goodness, the knowledge sees supreme soul in everyone, the action performed without attachment, love and hatred, the performer has no ego, lot of enthusiasm, no waver on success or failure. In passion the knowledge see different people in bodies, actions are performed with great effort to satisfy the desires, performer is always worried about fruitive results, envy and greedy. In ignorance, knowledge sees darkness in everything, the action performed with illusion and disregard, the performer is cheating, lazy and materialistic.

In goodness, the understanding helps to find the right actions, the determination is unbreakable and oriented with clean faith, the happiness that starts as tough one and ends as pure one. In passion, the understanding is not able to differentiate the right and wrong actions, the determination based on results/economic/religious/sense gratification, and happiness based on senses, the start as pure and end as Poisson. In Ignorance, the understanding is the wrong actions will be perceived as right ones, determination is based on illusion, dreaming and unintelligent, the happiness is from beginning to end it's of delusion. These three characters affect everyone. Being purified by intelligence, self control, who performs duties , controls food, removes false pride, ego, who lives in peace can understand me , as I am , the supreme god, they in full consciousness serve me and live with me. Though engaged in all kind of activities, my devotee achieves me. The one who is conscious on me, who always thinks on me, I am there to help him cross this life and he will be never lost. As supreme god,

I am there in everyone, just they need to surrender to me, and then I take care of them. The most confidential knowledge is, always think about me, worship, surrender all results to me, by this you will come to me, without fail, I promise this. The one who understand this should tell to others and the one, who hears this with full faith and follows it, will reach me. After hearing, this Arjuna told to supreme god, that he understands his duty and ready to perform it now.

Sanjaya explained all those wording to Dhritarashtra and told him, that these wordings made him stand and he always like to remember them in his mind. Then Arjuna went to the battle and the Pandavas have won the great battle.

"Our Life: I always wonder why a human should perform an action without result. It may be good for talk but not for real life! And thinking of growing in life, making money and keeping the family happy is the ultimate purpose for living, how can I leave those and lead a life? Gita is not for a common person... that is the thinking I had and may be you also had at the beginning; now to some level we both have our answers.... Performing action is the key for us to live, we as common people can't stop performing action, but we can cut the expectation on results, because the results lead to expectation and expectation leads to desires and desire leads misery and illusion. Some of us think, by doing action, we can wait, because god will give us the result... This also another expectation, but now it is on

god... Perform your duties and offer all the results to god, this is simpler for us. When our growth is important for others and we do not take pride, attach ourselves in that growth, then a growth is not harmful, it is again part of duty for us, as a person with such capability. However the moment, we think, it we who has done, and doing it, leading it, we are lost. Similarly as a common person, we all do activities to satisfy the sensual needs, however we should be able to distance them as we demand, and for that, it's important to surrender all this happenings to god. We cannot attach anything but only to supreme power, with all other things we can live, but with clarity they exist today and may not exist tomorrow. We can be there with children, wife, parents, brothers, and friends and with all the useful assets, but be clear, one day they will go out and we will go out from this life... However, we will never be left alone without god! The ultimate supreme power is always within you, so what else you need... Even if you die, even if your soul leaves, every moment he is there with you and finally you reach him...so what's there to worry! Surrender yourself to him, he will take care! (Do not get confused to which god I need to surrender, because one god may get angry if you surrender yourself with another god :)) The one supreme power of this universe is within you, and you are within him!!! With this run your life, perform your duties, leave the worries and detach yourself from pride, ego, and expectations"

CONCLUSION

You and I had our own interpretations, when we read this. You and I had our own imagination about Krishna and Arjuna, and some you have accepted, some you may have confronted. However, we both united in one part, that we both are from same supreme power and we both are part of it, here age never matters, money never matters, position never matters. By reading this or by writing this or by arguing this, we may not be completely changed from today to tomorrow, we might be still doing most of them in same way. However, I know that everything comes from him, including me, this will help me to handle elements in life. At the introduction, I was telling that I am searching for identity, now my search stopped, and I know who I am. Now, I do not feel lonely, even the loneliest time in my future, I know I will not be lonely. You may have completely different thoughts on what I wrote, it is fine. Because what I wrote is also given by him, what you think is also created by him; he is not someone who can be put in words. The words given here are triggers to us, but more than that every living being enjoys him within them, so you can describe him more than what is here! You can cherish him more than what is here! This is no conclusion, this a running experience. As a villager lives in a village, without seeing the world, with my limited abilities I tried to understand Gita in my own way to my capability and shared it, there could be pundit's who travelled across globe, have read line by line, word by word and done lot of research on Bhagavad Gita, they can find many errors in this compilation. However for a villager, who enjoys the humming of bird, who sees wonderful butterflies, and having healthy food, it may not matter what FM radio brings, what a operating system performs, what's the on time performance of a flight operator... does he really need to bother! It's finally turns out to be, how you perceive and live and what he had blessed for you!"

ABOUT THE AUTHOR

Vishnuvarthanan Moorthy (1979 - TBD by God) was born and brought up in India. I am just another common person in this world.

About my writing - The thoughts and the questions we have in our mind are extraordinary. Some of us decide to give a form by writing and communicating with others, whereas some decides to not to give. We all imagine so much in our mind and every time we imagine about something, we are able to simulate and visualize the happenings. However, most of the time of our thinking, imagination and visualization based on what we have seen, studied, experienced or viewed. Very rarely, we imagine something that is very new; otherwise, we just present them as new! This shows human mind is more pattern oriented and recency oriented. It means if you keep feeding the mind with good things and truthful things, by practice the human mind tend to perform good things. Books are one source for it and I write to communicate the truth, what I believe as good and what we together can like and share!

CPSIA information can be obtained
at www.ICGtesting.com
Printed in the USA
LVHW081737121118
596818LV00039B/1269/P